Toni MORRISON

JIM HASKINS

Toni MORRISON
The Magic of Words

A Gateway Biography
The Millbrook Press Brookfield, Connecticut

To Margaret Emily

Cover photograph courtesy of AP/Wide World Photos

Photographs courtesy of Sygma: p. 8 (© Michelina Pelletier); Corbis: p. 12; Birmingham Public Library Department of Archives and Manuscripts (catalog no. 20.42): p. 14; Black River Historical Society: pp. 15, 16, 19; ClassMates.Com Yearbook Archives: p. 20; Corbis/Bettmann-UPI: pp. 23, 37 (right); Moorland-Spingarn Research Center, Howard University Archives: p. 24; AP/Wide World Photos: pp. 27, 36 (right), 37 (left), 43, 44; © Matt Herron/Take Stock: p. 28; © Bettmann/Corbis: p. 32; The Schomburg Center, New York Public Library: pp. 35, 36 (left)

Published by The Millbrook Press, Inc.
2 Old New Milford Road
Brookfield, Connecticut 06804
www.millbrookpress.com

Library of Congress Cataloging-in-Publication Data
Haskins, James, 1941–
Toni Morrison: the magic of words / by Jim Haskins.
   p. cm.—(A Gateway biography)
Includes index.
ISBN 0-7613-1806-2 (lib. bdg.)
1. Morrison, Toni—Juvenile literature. 2. Novelists, American—20th century—Biography—Juvenile literature. 3. Afro-American women novelists—Biography—Juvenile literature. [1. Morrison, Toni. 2. Authors, American. 3. Women—Biography. 4. Afro-Americans—Biography.] I. Title. II. Series.
PS3563.O8749 Z675 2001
813'.54—dc21
[B]   00-032868

Contents

Toni MORRISON

Introduction

In November 1993, Toni Morrison won the Nobel Prize for literature. This famous international award is the highest honor for a writer. Morrison was the first African American woman to win this prize. She traveled to Stockholm, Sweden, to accept it.

Two weeks later, Morrison's house in Grand View-on-Hudson, New York, caught fire. She was lucky that her papers were not badly damaged. But she lost many other things. Family photographs, favorite houseplants, and her sons' school report cards all burned in the fire. About ten weeks after the fire, Morrison's mother died.

Toni Morrison began life in modest circumstances. This is the story of her overcoming economic, racial, and gender barriers to become the elegant and accomplished woman seen posing here after accepting the Nobel Prize for literature.

Morrison's greatest dream, greatest nightmare, and a great sorrow all happened to her in just three months. For a short time, her own life became like one of her stories. Joy bumps up against great tragedy in her stories. Luckily, for Morrison and for the rest of us who live ordinary lives, her stories are usually "bigger than life." She takes her readers to places that could never be. She writes about people you can only meet in stories, like a woman born with no belly button and a man who believes he can fly. She takes us on the kinds of wild adventures we would prefer to take only in our imaginations. The characters Toni Morrison creates and the things that happen to them move into a reader's mind and stay there. This is the mark of a true writer.

Chapter 1
Childhood

Toni Morrison was born black, female, and poor in a time when there were very few opportunities in the United States for someone like her. She has said that if she had lived the life that was expected of her, "I would have lived and died in somebody else's kitchen, on somebody's else's land, and never written a word."

When Toni Morrison was born, African Americans were second-class citizens. This was true throughout the country. It was true in Lorain, Ohio, where she grew up. But it was especially true in the South, where her parents had been born and raised. That is why they had left the South and settled in Ohio. Toni grew up hearing about the hatred and cruelty blacks suffered at the hands of Southern white people.

Toni Morrison's mother was named Ramah Willis Wofford. She was born on a farm in Alabama. She was one of seven children of sharecroppers who lived and worked on a white man's land. The Willis family was supposed to be able to keep some of the profits from the farming work they did. But the white

landowner always found a way to keep them in debt. He would charge high prices for seed and fertilizer and for rent on the house in which they lived. Toni's grandfather realized that he would never get out of debt to his white landlord. He left his family and went to the city of Birmingham. There, he found work as a jazz musician. Toni's grandmother remained on the farm with her seven children. But without her husband, she could not keep up the work on the farm. In 1906, she left the farm with all seven children and joined her husband in Birmingham. Life in Birmingham was still hard for blacks. But the family found more opportunities there than they had as sharecroppers.

Morrison's father, George Wofford, had grown up in Georgia. At that time, whites often murdered blacks. They were not arrested or tried in court for this crime. Lynching, a killing by a mob, used to be common in the South. As a child, Morrison's father saw such cruelty on the part of whites that he came to hate all white people. As soon as he was able, he left the South.

Toni Morrison has no pictures of her grandparents as her photographs were all destroyed in the 1993 fire. This, however, is a picture from the late 1890s showing a group of sharecroppers picking peanuts. Conditions were certainly better than those of slavery thirty years before—but for the average family, it was nearly impossible to break out of the cycle of poverty.

Birmingham, Alabama, shown here in 1906, the year of Toni's mother's arrival there, appears to be a land of golden opportunity compared to a sharecropper's life on a farm.

Hundreds of thousands of other blacks did the same. Most of them headed for Northern cities. Blacks were not treated as equals even in the North. But at least they didn't have to worry so much about being lynched.

Toni was born in Lorain, Ohio, in 1931. Her parents named her Chloe Anthony Wofford. She got the nickname Toni in college. Morrison is her married name. She was the second child and second daughter in her family. Two boys were born later. She jokes that she felt left out: She was not the oldest; she was not the first son; she was not the baby. "Feeling left out and trying to attract attention, I became the noisiest of them all," she says.[1]

Morrison was born in the time of the Great Depression. Many Americans were out of work. It was hard for them to feed and shelter their families. Morrison's father worked when he could as

This is the house where Chloe Anthony Wofford was born. Chloe was later nicknamed Toni in college, and then married a man named Morrison, thereby becoming Toni Morrison.

16

a shipyard welder. He also took odd jobs. During the Depression, he sometimes worked three jobs in order to take care of his family. Morrison's mother was a housewife. The family was very poor, but they were also very proud.

Says Morrison, "The world back then didn't expect much from a little black girl, but my father and mother certainly did."[2] Her parents made Morrison and her brothers and sisters feel proud of themselves. They taught them that being poor did not keep them from being special people.

Toni Morrison grew up in a black neighborhood that was largely separated from whites. It was a close-knit community. Everyone knew everyone else's business and cared about one another.

Music was important in that community and in Morrison's family. Her grandfather had been a jazz musician. Her parents and grandparents were fine musicians, although they could not read music. Morrison and her sisters and brothers took music

This is the downtown area of Lorain, Ohio, in the 1940s, during Morrison's teen years. The scene is typical of midwestern towns of the period, although few, if any, photographic records exist of the black ghettos that existed behind the main streets of such towns.

lessons. Morrison also loved dancing. For a long time, she wanted to be a dancer when she grew up.

Storytelling was another important part of life in the black community of Lorain, Ohio. People told stories of strength and courage in their families. They also told ghost stories and shared their dreams. Morrison's grandmother kept a dream book in which she wrote down the stories that came to her when she was sleeping.

Morrison's family was very religious. Her parents and grandmother read the Bible out loud. It contained wonderful stories. Toni Morrison loved the stories told by the adults in her family and the stories in the Bible. She was very young when she discovered the magic of books. Her mother belonged to a book club when book clubs were just beginning. "The security I felt, the pleasure, when new books arrived was immense," Morrison recalls.[3]

Reading played a part in one of Morrison's early experiences with prejudice. When she was in fifth grade, a new boy enrolled in her class. His family had just arrived in the United States, and he didn't speak English. He sat next to Morrison in class. He listened to her read out loud. He followed the words on the page

The Lorain Public Library was no doubt an important place for young Toni Morrison, who was the first child in her kindergarten class to learn to read. Her early childhood love of books has remained with her throughout her life.

and so learned to read himself. But by that time, he had also learned that white Americans looked down on black Americans. It no longer mattered to him that she had taught him to read. What mattered more was that she was somebody he could be better than. Morrison says, "I remember the moment he found out that I was black—a nigger. . . . That's the moment when he belonged; that was his entrance. Every immigrant knew he would not come at the very bottom. He had to come above at least one group—and that was us."4

When Morrison was thirteen years old, she started working part-time. She used the money she earned to help out with the family expenses. She would go to the home of a local white woman after school and clean for three hours. She remembers, "You got to work these gadgets that I never had at home: vacuum cleaners."5

As she worked, Morrison would hum her favorite songs or daydream. Sometimes she daydreamed about becoming a great dancer. It did not occur to her to daydream about being a writer.

On graduating from high school, Morrison could have gone to work as a full-time maid. That's what many young black women did. But her parents had bigger plans for their children. They worked and saved so their children could go to college.

By the time she graduated from high school, Toni, then known as Chloe, was a beautiful young woman already showing signs of promise. She is shown here in her high-school yearbook as the treasurer of her senior class.

Chapter 2
College, Teaching and Marriage

Toni Morrison graduated from Lorain High School in 1949. Her parents helped her pay the tuition to Howard University in Washington, D.C. This all-black college was founded by the United States Congress in 1867. When Morrison was a student at Howard, Washington, D.C., was as segregated as any other Southern city. She had to sit in the back of city buses. If she had tried to eat at a white restaurant, she would have been refused service. The District of Columbia had separate drinking fountains for "Whites" and "Colored." It also had separate public library branches. Like other students at Howard, Morrison avoided white Washington, D.C., as much as possible.

The entry gate to Howard University seemed to symbolize two things for those students fortunate enough to be enrolled. It was a welcoming entrance into a new world of intellectual achievement and future potential—but it also was a barrier that at least temporarily locked out the bitter hatred and prejudice of the surrounding environs.

Howard and its surrounding community were like an island in a white sea. Students stayed on or near the campus to avoid being treated badly by whites. But Morrison did not feel as if she escaped segregation at Howard. The university was supposed to prepare young black people to succeed in the world. But it taught the history of whites. It did not teach about the contributions blacks had made to American and world culture. She was also disturbed by the importance placed on skin color and family status. Most male students at Howard chose to date women who were light-skinned, with wavy hair. Most female students chose their friends on the same basis.

Some of Morrison's happiest times were with the Howard Unity Players, the school's acting group. The students in that group were more concerned with her talent than with the way she looked or where her family came from. She traveled across the country with the Howard players. With the group, she had her first experiences in the South. She saw and felt the discrimination against blacks that had caused her own parents to leave.

Morrison was a woman of many talents. As a child she loved to dance, and while her writing talents were emerging during the years at Howard, she was an active member of the school's acting group. Here she is shown in a production of Shakespeare's King Richard III.

While at Howard, Chloe Anthony Wofford became Toni Wofford. Her friends had a hard time pronouncing her name. They thought Chloe was a strange name. They began to call her "Toni," short for Anthony. She continued to be Chloe to her family.

Morrison majored in English at Howard. She received her bachelor of arts degree in 1953. She then went to graduate school at Cornell University in Ithaca, New York.

In 1954, while she was at Cornell, a momentous event occurred. After a long campaign in the courts, an organization called the National Association for the Advancement of Colored People (NAACP) finally managed to win a landmark legal ruling. The United States Supreme Court, in the case of *Brown* v. *Board of Education*, declared that "separate but equal" schools were unconstitutional. A majority of the justices on the court felt that the United States Constitution never meant for American citi-

While Toni Morrison was pursuing her studies in Ithaca, New York, an event occurred in Washington, D.C., that would forever affect the ability of other black children to follow in her footsteps. The court ruled against segregated schooling based on the challenge of Linda Brown against the Board of Education of Topeka [Kansas]. This 1964 photo shows Brown standing in front of the school that had refused to admit her thirteen years earlier because of her race.

zens to attend segregated schools. If the Supreme Court said blacks should be able to go to school with whites, then someday blacks should also have other equal rights. They should be able to drink from the same water fountains, ride in the same bus seats, vote like whites, and other things.

Toni Morrison received her master of arts degree from Cornell University in 1955. She then looked for a job teaching English. At the time, white colleges and black colleges were still segregated. She applied to black colleges for her first teaching job. She was hired as an instructor in English at Texas Southern University, a black college in Houston. She stayed there two years. In 1957, she got a job as an instructor in English at Howard University and moved back to Washington, D.C.

Three years had passed since the Supreme Court decision declaring "separate but equal" schools unconstitutional. But little had changed in the nation's segregated communities—not in the schools and not in other areas of life. The Supreme Court had declared that segregated school districts should integrate their

Many of the leaders of what came to be known as the Civil Rights Movement can be seen in this photograph of a march from Selma to Montgomery, Alabama, in favor of voting rights: James Bevel, Andrew Young, Ralph Bunche, Martin Luther King Jr., Coretta Scott King, Bayard Rustin, A. Philip Randolph, and Ralph Abernathy.

schools "with all deliberate speed." For Southerners who were furious about the court's decision, that meant "not in my lifetime."

But Southern blacks were tired of segregation. They believed that the law of the land was now on their side. They began to take action to win their rights. In Montgomery, Alabama, a seamstress named Rosa Parks got tired of giving up her seat on the city bus when white people were standing. One evening, she refused to give her seat to a white man. She was arrested and taken to jail. The black citizens of Montgomery protested her arrest. They refused to ride the buses for more than a year. Leaders of the boycott sued the city in the federal courts. Finally, at the end of 1956, the United States Supreme Court ruled segregation on public transportation unconstitutional. A young minister in Montgomery named Martin Luther King Jr. was one of the leaders of the boycott. He joined with other Southern black ministers to form the Southern Christian Leadership Conference (SCLC). The SCLC began to campaign for the right to vote for blacks in the South.

Toni Morrison returned to Washington, D.C., just as the SCLC began that campaign. She did not see much difference in the way blacks were treated in Washington, D.C. But, like other blacks, she was hopeful that segregation might one day end there and elsewhere in the South.

Not long after returning to Howard, Toni met Harold Morrison. He was an architect who had been born in Jamaica. Like Toni, he was raised to feel proud of his heritage. He was especially proud that Jamaica had been the birthplace of Marcus Garvey.

Garvey was an important black leader in the early years of the twentieth century. He believed that blacks would never enjoy equal rights in a largely white society. He urged blacks to go to Africa, the homeland of their ancestors. After he left Jamaica for the United States, the membership of his organization, the United Negro Improvement Association (UNIA), increased greatly. Toni's father had been a follower of Garvey. But United States authorities considered Garvey's ideas dangerous. In 1916, he was arrested on charges of mail fraud and deported back to Jamaica. He was unable to rebuild his movement.

Toni Wofford and Harold Morrison fell in love and were married in 1958. Their first son, Harold Ford Morrison, was born in 1962. Slade Kevin Morrison, their second son, was born four years later.

Toni Morrison stopped teaching in order to be a housewife and mother. But she was bored. She needed to talk to other adults. She joined a local writers group so she could share her passion for literature. She was not thinking about becoming a writer.

Morrison loved to read and hear and tell stories. But she had never thought about trying to write books. One reason was that there were very few books written by blacks. This was especially true of novels. Many blacks were talented writers, but publishing companies were owned by whites. They did not believe white readers would be interested in books about black life. And they

As Toni Morrison's interest in writing began to mature, she had virtually no role models. Only one African American had become a well-known author at that time: Richard Wright. His Native Son, *a novel about a black teenager in Chicago who killed a white girl, had caused a huge reaction when it was published in 1940.*

did not believe there were enough educated black people around to read books written by blacks.

Back in the 1920s, many Southern blacks had moved to the North to escape the violent racism of the South. At that time, quite a few black authors had managed to get their books published. But many of these authors and their books had been forgotten.

While in the writers' group, Toni Morrison began a short story about a young girl growing up in an all-black community in Ohio. She was too busy being a wife and mother to give much of her time to writing it. She thought of writing as a hobby.

But soon Toni Morrison gave up on being a wife. She left her husband and moved back with her family in Lorain, Ohio. She and Harold Morrison later divorced. She felt badly about ending her marriage. Her mother, her grandmother, and even her great-grandmother had enjoyed good marriages. Sadly, Toni Morrison did not. She does not talk about her marriage very often. She has said, "He knew better about his life, but not about mine. I had to stop and say, let me start again and see what it is like to be a grown-up."[1]

Toni Morrison never remarried. She chose not to. She worried about how her sons would react to a stepfather. She also enjoyed having the freedom to make her own decisions.

Chapter 3
Editor

By the time Toni Morrison left her husband, major changes in race relations had taken place in the United States. The nonviolent civil rights movement in the South caused the federal government to declare segregation illegal in all areas of life. The Civil Rights Act of 1964 guaranteed equal rights in many areas of life. The Voting Rights Act of 1965 declared that all citizens had the right to vote. At the same time, schools began to include more black history in their lessons. Publishers of school textbooks began adding more black history into their social studies texts.

Toni Morrison took a job with a textbook publisher based in Syracuse, New York. She and her sons moved there. Three years later, she was promoted to senior editor at Random House in New York City. She and her sons moved to New City, New York, in the suburbs of New York City. There were very few black editors at major publishing houses at the time. There were still very few books by black authors being published. As she gained respect and power at Random House, Morrison began to encourage black authors. She was especially interested in women writers.

The number of black women writers whose work had been published in the United States by 1967 could be counted on two hands. The first was Phillis Wheatley, born in Africa and taken to Boston, Massachusetts, as a small child in 1761. Her first volume of poems was published in England in 1793. It was the first book published by an American black and only the second book published by an American woman. Not until 1861 was the first novel published by a black American woman. Harriet Jacobs wrote a story of her own life in slavery titled *Incidents in the Life of a Slave Girl.* She published it under a pseudonym, Linda Brent.

Zora Neale Hurston stood out among the other writers of what came to be known as the Harlem Renaissance because she was from the rural South, because she chose to write ethnic folktales, and mainly because she was a woman.

In Toni Morrison's lifetime, four African American women had managed to get books published. Zora Neale Hurston had published novels and plays during the 1930s. Ann Petry had

Ann Petry wrote three well-received novels in the 1940s: The Street, Country Place, *and* The Narrows. *She wrote stories not only of black oppression, but also of black survival.*

Gwendolyn Brooks was the first black American to win a Pulitzer Prize, for her second poetry collection, Annie Allen. *The poems are about a young black girl growing up in the early 1940s.*

published a novel in 1945. In 1950, poet Gwendolyn Brooks became the first African American to win the Pulitzer Prize for her book of poetry, *Annie Allen*. The prize is named for the newspaper publisher Joseph Pulitzer. It is awarded each year in a variety of genres of writing that also include fiction, nonfiction, and newspaper reporting. In 1959, Paule Marshall's *Brown Girl,*

Paule Marshall's works were well received in the 1960s, among them Daughters, *a novel about a young black professional, periodically distracted from her hectic life in Manhattan by thoughts of her past.*

Lorraine Hansberry became famous for her play A Raisin in the Sun (1959) *about a black family's stuggles to leave the Chicago ghetto. The play won the New York Drama Critics Circle Award.*

Brown Stones was published. That same year, Lorraine Hansberry's *A Raisin in the Sun* became the first play by a black woman to be produced on Broadway.

Toni Morrison decided that there should be more novels by black women. As senior editor at a major publishing house, she could help make that happen. Soon, she became a novelist herself.

Chapter 4
Writer

While she was still working as an editor of textbooks in Syracuse, New York, Morrison started writing again. She returned to the short story she had started in the writers' workshop in Washington, D.C., several years before. She worked and worked on the story of the little black girl who believes that all her problems will be solved if only she can have blue eyes. After moving to the job at Random House in New York City, Morrison shared her story with another editor. He told her she should try to make it a novel.

Morrison was a single mother with a full-time job as an editor. She did not have much time to write. She says now that she "stole" the time. She got up very early in the morning to write before her children awoke. On the packed subways on her way to and from work, she thought about characters and situations. She also wrote on weekends when the boys were out playing with their friends. In the summers, she sent her sons to stay with her parents in Ohio. While they were gone, she devoted her free time to writing.

Morrison did not tell anyone at Random House that she was writing a book. When she finished the manuscript, she gave it to the editor friend who had encouraged her. He bought it for publication.

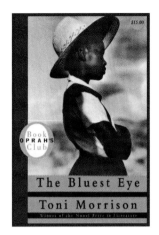

Morrison was nearly forty years old when her first book, *The Bluest Eye,* was published in 1970. She was shocked when she saw the name on the cover. She recalls, "They had the wrong name: Toni Morrison. My name is Chloe Wofford. Toni's a nickname."[1] She had sent the manuscript in under that name because her editor friend knew her by that name. She had been called by that name by her friends since college. Still, it was strange to see that name on the cover of her first book.

Morrison included many of her own experiences in *The Bluest Eye.* The story is set in the town of Lorain, Ohio. One of the characters, Pauline, lives in a shack and hates it. Then she goes to work for a white family with a beautiful house and loves it. The story features a girl who is eleven years old in 1941. Morrison herself was eleven years old in that year. The girl, Pecola Breedlove, is trying to find her own identity. But her family and community put barriers in her way. She finally escapes the ugliness of her life and her belief that she herself is ugly. She goes mad and decides that she has magically been given blue eyes. The book was written like poetry.

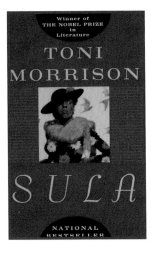

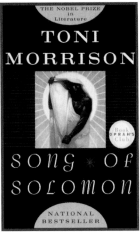

That first book was followed three years later by *Sula*. It, too, was a short book set in an all-black community in the Midwest. It was also written in beautiful, poetic language. *Sula* was widely reviewed and praised.

Four years after *Sula* was published, *Song of Solomon* was issued. While writing this book, Morrison came to feel that she was a real writer, that writing was a central part of her life. "Not to say that other women haven't said it all along," she adds, "but for a woman to say 'I am a writer' is difficult."[2] Sadly, Morrison's father did not live to see that. He died shortly before the book was published.

One of the characters in *Song of Solomon* believes he can fly. The book itself is a swooping flight of the imagination. It won both the National Book Critics Circle Award and the American Academy and Institute of Arts and Letters Award in 1977. That same year, it was also the first novel by a black writer to be a Book-of-the-Month-Club selection since Richard Wright's *Native Son* nearly forty years earlier. *Song of Solomon* established Toni Morrison as a major writer.

Tar Baby was published in 1981, four years after *Song of Solomon*. It is the story of a love affair between a black model who is ashamed to be black and a black man who is proud to be. Morrison took her title, *Tar Baby*, from Southern American folklore. In the "Uncle Remus" story of the same name, Brer Fox decides to outwit Brer Rabbit. He creates a baby figure out of tar. Brer Rabbit is caught up in the sticky substance. Toni Morrison's *Tar Baby* was not as successful as her earlier novels. It did not win any awards.

In 1985, Toni Morrison resigned her position as a senior editor at Random House. She had worked at that publishing company for eighteen years. She had helped many African American writers, especially women, to get published. They included Toni Cade Bambara, Alice Walker, and Gayl Jones. Toni Morrison took a job teaching humanities at the State University of New York at Albany. Teaching gave her more time to write. But finding the time to write was as difficult as when she had had young children at home because now that she was a major writer, she received many invitations to give lectures and make appearances around the country.

In 1987, Morrison's fifth novel, *Beloved*, was published. It took longer to write than her earlier novels because it was about slavery. She had done a lot of research into the history of slavery. It had been very painful for her to do that research. As she said in 1989, "I had this terrible reluctance about dwelling on that era. Then I realized I didn't know anything about it, really. And I was overwhelmed by how long it was. Suddenly the time—three hundred years—began to drown me. Three hundred years—think about that. Now, that's not a war, that's generation after generation."[3]

In fact, slavery was so painful to read and write about that Morrison wondered if anyone would read her book. She recalled, "I thought this has got to be the least read of all the books I'd written because it is about something that the characters don't want to remember, I don't want to remember, black people don't want to remember, white people don't want to remember. I mean, it's national amnesia."[4]

Beloved is based on the true story of a slave woman who murdered her own child rather than bring her into a life of slavery. Years later, the ghost of the child returns. In spite of Morrison's

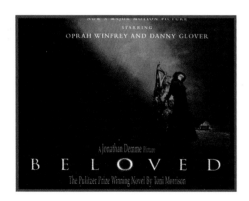

fears, the book was widely read and praised. It was nominated for both a National Book Award and a National Book Critics Circle Award. In 1988, it won the Pulitzer Prize for fiction. In 1998, *Beloved* was made into a movie produced by Oprah Winfrey.

In 1989, Morrison became Professor of the Humanities at Princeton University in Princeton, New Jersey. Her sixth novel, *Jazz*, was published in 1992. Following its publication, Toni Morrison won the Nobel Prize.

Each year since 1901, a committee in Sweden has awarded prizes for outstanding achievement in five areas. They are physics, chemistry, medicine, and literature, as well as for the promotion of international peace. These cash prizes were established by the will of Alfred Nobel (1833–1896), a Swedish chemist and inventor. Over the years, the Nobel Prize in literature had been awarded to a few Americans. It had never been given to an African American. When Toni Morrison won the prize in 1993,

Toni Morrison poses in the offices of her publisher to publicize the release of Beloved. *The publisher felt that the book was her greatest novel, in fact one of the all-time great American novels. Morrison chafed at the notion at the time, but the book was received as a literary landmark.*

One must wonder what Toni Morrison was thinking in the dramatic moment in 1993 when she became the first black woman to receive the Nobel Prize for literature. She is shown here accepting the prize from Sweden's King Carl XVI Gustav.

she was the first African American to do so. She was also the first African American woman to win a Nobel Prize of any sort. In earlier years, Dr. Ralph Bunche and Dr. Martin Luther King Jr. had won the Nobel Prize for peace.

Morrison stepped to the podium on the stage of the Swedish Academy to deliver her acceptance speech. She carried herself with the regal dignity that her parents had taught her. She spoke about the importance of language. When she was finished, the audience gave her a standing ovation. And then, for the first time anyone could remember, the audience stood for a second ovation. Morrison's father would have been proud. But he would not be alone. At long last, the little black girl from Lorain, Ohio, was claimed by every American. Wrote the critic John Leonard in *The New York Times*, "There's never been such majesty. I wasn't the only wet-eyed New York smarty-pants proud to be a citizen of whatever country Toni Morrison comes from."

Source Notes

CHAPTER 1
1. *Time*, January 19, 1998, p. 68.
2. *Time*, January 19, 1998, p. 68.
3. *The New York Times Magazine*, September 11, 1984, p. 73.
4. *Time* On line, May 22, 1989, p. 1.
5. *The New York Times Magazine*, September 11, 1984, p. 73.

CHAPTER 2
1. *The Art of Fiction*, p. 99.

CHAPTER 4
1. *The New York Times Magazine*, September 11, 1984, p. 74.
2. *The Art of Fiction*, p. 96.
3. Bonnie Angelo, "The Pain of Being Black," *Time*, May 22, 1989.
4. Ibid., p. 3.

Further Information

The Nobel Foundation has created a Nobel Electronic Museum on the World Wide Web (www.nobel.se), where visitors can read on-line autobiographies, accounts of individual awards, and some of the acceptance speeches, including Toni Morrison's.

Index